I Always Think I've Seen It All

Aleksandra Kowalczuk

BookLeaf
Publishing

India | USA | UK

Presentation by *BookLeaf Publishing*

Web: www.bookleafpub.com

E-mail: info@bookleafpub.com

ISBN: 978-93-5744-801-7

First edition 2022

DEDICATION

Dla kochanej babci,

prawdziwej poetce.

ACKNOWLEDGEMENT

Without my inspirations, these poems would not exist. Y'all know who you are.

Thank you, thank you, thank you.

PREFACE

This book is about love.
Platonic love, romantic love, family love, self
love.
It's about the lack of love.
For some, that's hatred, for others, indifference.
For me, this collection of poems was created to
help understand these different types of love I've
experienced over the years.

To future poems to come.
Enjoy.

The Heart's Journey

At first, so full
So new and clean
So pure, so red
All yet unseen.

Then everyday
Miasmic truths,
You learn it's more
Than deaths and births.

You learn of hardships
Crushes deep,
You learn there's more
Then restful sleep.

You learn things hurt,
Not physically,
But ways need fixed
In therapy.

You find Sartre
Within the stacks
Then you expand
Filling the cracks.

You think you've found
Something to fill
But realize
It's empty still.

Each D or F,
Each lifeless glance,
Each "only friend",
Each "I don't dance";

They all cut slow.
Not always deep
But more and more…
Blood starts to creep.

It oozes red,
It flows just slow
Enough so you
Don't feel it flow.

But years pass by.
You don't suspect.
Until it's found
Your heart is wrecked.

For every day,
Felt or suppressed,
It never gave

Your heart a rest.

It's crippled now,
At once, serene,
By people that
It has been seen.

The Light Came Up
Too Quickly

The light came up too quickly
And just like that you're gone.

I have to wait another day
And yet another one,
To hold you tightly once again
To lie down on your chest.
I never knew the comfort
It would bring.
It would be best
If you just never left again
And even though I love
That goodbye kiss at 4am,
There's more that I think of.

I think what it you never left
Whatever would we do?
Like thrifting, drinking coffee late,
Much later than we should.
We'd walk the dog down to the park
Not holding hands, of course
Because you know that mine get sweaty

When I have you close.

I never bore, I never tire
Somehow, when I'm with you.
I'd never think to give you up.
You make me feel less blue.

So while I drink my coffee
On your front steps, just today,
You'll be in bed
And I won't have to ask
For you to stay.

A Poem, For You

I never had a sibling.
I never loved like that.
But you have come the closest
To feeling like I had.

There's rooms inside my heart
So many, big and small,
And you have got one of the biggest
Coolest, full of color.
It's got so many posters
Of bands we've to discover.
The door is big and bold,
Just like we've always been.
And so many old poems;
They always make me grin.
It's got a coffee station,
With 20 kinds of tea
And homemade almond milk
That's made by you and me.
There's vintage record players
And records to go with,
And books of our adventures
Some fact and some just myth.

With your studded boots,

And your white lace dress
You're always dressed to impress.
You've impressed me the most
Not with the clothes
But with the heart,
The change I've seen since we've been apart,
Since school,
Since we've both moved,
Since we've met men,
Since we've learned to groove.

She'll be gone,
They say.
But I don't think of it that way.
You'll be free.
That's what they don't see.

The land of opportunity for you
That's the west coast
That's the best coast
For my little Alexa.

Eye For an Eye,
Heart For a Heart

Well,
Here you are.
Making me feel like shit again.
Just because you lost your man.

Are you mad cuz I'm getting some?
Are you mad cuz I get to cum?
Are you mad that he's more fun
Then any boy that you've been on?

Go find your world.
Good luck, my friend.
I'll always be here till our end.

But if you try to mess with me
I'll lose all friendly dignity.
I won't be bigger, won't be wise
Might hear some things that you'll despise.

I love you.
That will never change
But hearts are big enough for more.

Don't take it all
Just for yourself
You don't own me just cuz I score.

Is jealousy the thorn you have?
Or fear, or sadness?
Maybe both
Whatever it is
It's none of mine.
So I should stay out of your line.

You see?
You see how easy that was?
To mind my own business?
To stay in my lane?
You make me question my own mind
Just one more time,
Then you're to blame.

Heartbreak Hotel
Native

Why don't you fuck her anymore?
You tired?
You bored?
Have dark haired brunettes fulfilled all you
needed?
Have her whips and chains done left you
defeated?
So you don't need me in your bed anymore?
With all those Greek sisters you've settled the
score?

You say that I ask you too many questions.
Well, I'm just trying to understand.
Cuz how can you double dip in all the cups
Then say, please baby, give me your hand.

They all look alike
But they all look like me
All skinny and clean, their dress ironed.
Am I just like that girl
From that post from last week

With the caption, "Boys, I'll get you fired".

You reach out to me
Every once in a while
When your inventory's hit a slump.
You sell yourself off
Charging twice the amount
Like a relationship pump and dump.

How is it that I fall every time
For your heart-breakingly evil scheme.
And the worst thing
Is that you don't see for yourself
That your actions have this darker theme.
You play with these girls like you play Call of
Duty,
Whether on your screen of real life.
And what keeps me up late in the dark of the
night
Is that one day, you'll heart break your wife.

You're a walking tornado,
Always hurting the ones
That are on this blue earth just to live.
So go play your games
With those boys in the field
A Heartbreak Hotel pure native.

I Lost My Watch

I lost my watch
But I look at yours all the time.
I look at you all the time.

I've never met
Someone who gives me the sheets.
One that buys all the best treats
So I'd be all set.
All cozy in bed
Watching movies instead
Of the drinks and the smokes.
It all seems like a joke.

There are days I feel alone
Knowing you're on your way.
My trust was betrayed
So many times.
You can try your best
But what's lost is lost.

I'm lucky our paths have crossed
And I have this watch now.
Please don't be offended
I always have ended
Things first.

It's the worst.

But this time,
The watch goes with my style.
I feel it may be worth my while.

It's Ok I Get It, You Just Think He's Prettier Than Me

I found a love I think is real
I know exactly how you feel.

When you found him I felt the same
No longer were we the same brain
We still hung out, got coffee, pie,
But he's the apple of your eye.

He left some scars in rooms of heart
Some walls and strings got pulled apart
And through it all I held your hand
And helped you when you couldn't stand.

And now he says
I'm free tomorrow.
And you don't care about my sorrow.
I'll eat some ice cream
Drink some wine
And put on dances by Divine.

Don't You See That You Are Nothing

Don't you see that you have nothing
Not a soul who swears by you,
Not a comrade. Filled with stuffing
Is the soul they thought they knew.

People change, that much is true
Cross the borders, oceans too.
But location shouldn't disimprove
The relations you have to the ones you choose.

What a lonely plot you weave
Sitting up there with your staff and breve.
Will you be ready when no one bows,
Because what comes up, must come down.

What a waste to see such a soul
Who had everything, you know.
Fall into a deep, dark hole
The devil himself wouldn't wish to go.

Diss Or Piss

Such harsh words
"You're no cool"
Changed since we
Were back in school

Now you skate
And smoke
And hate
When'd you turn to shit from great?

Role models you have a plenty
Never say "get lit" or "venti"
Never stay on top of trends
"Me and Billie should be friends!!!"

Academia - not your scene
"In the real world, they'll be green"
I speak fucking foreign tongues
All you do is fill up lungs.

Hate your school
Hate your friends
Hate the fact that youth once ends
Yet you never take advantage

Though you call yourself a "savage"

"You don't know the shit I've done"
Babe, I know you. You've done none.
You just sit and write in darkness
Hoping you will find a compass.

Get a call, a wallflower,
'Cuz you lost a follower
"I once had this friend, you know
Now she clicked unfollow. Hoe."

Validation from the outside
Never ends up well.
You'll die lonely, so sad. Boo hoo,
Go cry in your own cell.

If you think
Friends can't divorce
Oh honey, are you wrong.

Cuz I'm about to leave your ass
Though you don't know what's wrong.

Just This Once

You bail again
I'm stale again
I dye my hair to green
Unintentionally
I'm mad at you
Exceptionally

Yet what do I do?
I text it's ok
Cuz I'd want the same
From you in this way

You know,
It's so hard
To say this kindness
It's all of this mindfulness
My therapist says

I'll watch that new show
I wanted to start
Without you
Just out of spite
Just this once
Then
Give you a hug

Crybaby

How much can a person cry?

I cried this morning.
I cried at work.
I even cried in my dream.

I often wake up crying,
In the morning,
In the middle of the night.

They say it's chemicals in my brain,
I say it's that the world's insane.
We mask our feelings to be nice.
We view emotions as a vice.

When we are mad, we kick and scream;
Make mother's say "don't make a scene!"
When we're adults and kick and scream;
The doctors say we must be seen.

We punish dogs for barking and we punish cats
for fear,
When really all they're doing is protecting what
is dear.

Why do we talk to therapists when we should
talk to moms,
And dads and brothers, sons and boyfriends,
husbands, sisters, wives.

It makes us feel like we are crazy
All we want to be heard.
And when we feel like talking most,
We never say a word.

To Greta

You're more home than family
More home than my own man
No coffee shop, bar or piano lounge can
Give me that same feeling as I get
When you make yourself some tea and say
"You want some too?"

We drive down those country roads
Marilyn road crosses here
We could be going to visit Hades,
I wouldn't care, long as you're near.

I can find any man,
Any woman to take place in my heart
But you will never depart.

To Lupe

I didn't mean to pry
I didn't mean to cry.
But it was all the drugs
And you, I can't deny.

missu

You hurt me in my dream
Then again tomorrow day.
I should have seen it coming
When you said that you would stay.
These backwards thoughts,
They never go away.

I know that it's been said
So many times before,
But this time
It just feels so real
The situation is ideal.
And even when you make me mad
I still find reasons to be glad.

I'm on the verge of breaking up
Every day of my life.
Cuz what if I miss you too much
And it will break my heart?

I know they say that absence
It can make the heart grow strong.
But I have found the opposite,
I think that they're all wrong.

So please don't hurt
My gentle soul
And I'll make sure that yours is whole.

Lucille

The old fortune teller Lucille
Lived on the fourth floor on McNeal
With a bright glowing sign
That was seen from aboard
A big freighter made out of steel.

It was called the old SS Revenge
It opened its sails far and wide
In search for the souls that had ever done wrong
Under the cover of night.

Old Johnny onboard the Revenge
Had seen the sign from the deck
The night was as thick as pain and molasses
The water was quiet as death.

He gave it a second glance
Though never had done it before,
Because of two eyes that longingly shot
Like rifles, two bullets from shore.

His soul got pulled into port.
His body followed with ease.
The sailors all went to the bar to get numb
But Johnny, he wanted to feel.

The steps to the siren were steep
But with every step he could feel
His feet getting lighter, his thoughts getting
brighter
He started to feel the relief.

The room was enthralled in all smoke
With one small table and chair
In which, who'd have sat but the lady in black
With an all knowing, green eyed, deep stare.

He said, "Witch, I am too weak,
To walk, to drink and to sleep
Because of the fear that I gave to the men
Who have hurt others so easily.

"I take a part of my hurt
And give it to those who deserved
The pain they recieved for getting away
With a sentence they never got served."

"I don't know why I do these things
When then I get punished for the same
But I found myself on the old SS Revenge
When I woke up from sleep one dark day.

"Now others, they go drown themselves
In liquor, and wine and beer

But why would I numb myself any more
When all I want to do is feel?"

The wise green-eyed woman looked close
Straight through the man's unconscious soul
And saw a good person who couldn't escape
From his own self dug guilty hole.

"The guilt that you feel way deep down,
Proves the good you have deep inside
Though buried beneath coal, dust and dark
sheaths
Has not had the chance to have died."

"It's hard to move on from a life
That's filled with revenge here and there
But I never believed forgiveness was for me
Till I saw you sitting in this chair."

"All it takes is ones who believe
That change is a thing you achieve.
Not a thing that comes easy. It makes your head
dizzy.
The person you were, you must grieve.

"I always say love is the deed.
But loving yourself is the key
To forgive yourself for the things you have done
And finally set your soul free."

Johnny left green-eyed Lucille that day
And never looked back at his stay
At the SS Revenge. Now he has the chance
To live out his life the right way.

Mantra For Bad Days

It seems like everyone
Just keeps on getting in my way.
They yell so much
They talk so loud
It's so unneeded.

Please just stop
Can you just not
Kill off my vibe?
Because it took
So long
To bribe the gods to get here.

And Yet

So out of life and out of touch
I wish it didn't hurt so much

Peace slips away, so hard to clutch
I wish it didn't hurt so much

It often seems, so little gain
There's little breath and too much pain

The dark is getting hard to reign
There's little breath and too much pain

I run, I shout, I please, I kneel
I close my eyes, and still I feel

I never had much time to heal
I close my eyes, and still I feel

When I felt broke, when I felt tossed
When my heart fell with winter's frost

I held it close. At every cost.
Hope was one thing I never lost.

Written In Pen

You said you couldn't put me
In your calendar in pen
And that you'd pencil me in
Just like any other friend.
You cancel on our plans
When you are feeling very low
And that I understand,
I have that heavy feeling known.

But to me you are everything
What I look to each day.
A text, a call
Or even post,
Listen to what you say.
I hang on every word
Like it was in some sacred text
Although you don't think twice
When you respond to my rare sext.

I paint and write and sing
To get you out from way down deep
Because you have ingrained yourself.
For months now, you let steep.

I guess nothing will help

To get me to stop thinking bout
You all the time,
Just say I'm fine
Because I am too proud.

Why do you never say you love me?
I just have to guess
And it depends upon the day;
I feel it in my chest.
I feel my heart beat harder
Or I don't feel it at all
It feels like I know you
Then I feel like I hit a wall.

So please just say
That I'll be written in your book in pen.
Because I can't stand the unknown
Am I your love or friend?

Everyday I Wait

On Monday I wait for Tuesday,
Because Tuesdays we get food.
After Tuesday comes the weekend,
Saturdays bring up my mood.
I stay over until Sunday,
Sunday morning you leave soon
After sunup, I stay late
I leave with sun, you leave with moon.

You kiss me right before you leave
And if you didn't I'd be mad
The day you stop's the day I'll know
That you love me less, just a tad.
It's just the same as when you get
Confused when I don't say hello.
Without the hug or even kiss,
I don't think you would let me go.

I don't care what plays on the radio
When I leave to go home.
If I leave in the morning
Then you text me all day long.
I get mad when there's videos
That I don't think are good
Because I can't send them to you

And can't share my good mood.

I hear the Smiths and don't get sad
Because you like them too.
And when he sings his sad jigs
There's no tears, cuz I have you.
I even made a playlist:
Songs that make me think of you
But then I get embarrassed listening
A love-sick fool.

On your brown bedside table
There's a stack of notes I wrote
You kept them in a pile
Like a charming anecdote.
I leave them in your pockets,
In your pill case, in your shoes
Some might have gotten chewed up
By a cute dog on the loose.

Don't Let Me Get Old

Don't let me get old and I'll do the same.
Don't let me stand at the alter my name.
Those fools will throw flowers
Please don't catch them
Cuz there's more to life than a ring on your hand

Don't let me get old and I'll do the same
Don't let all those bookshelves fill up just for
gain
And don't let my mind be attached by a chain
To that alma mater you just know by name

Don't let me get old and I'll do the same
Run out with wet hair and into the rain
And yell like my mother, just let me feel mad
For things that have never really been that bad

Don't let me get old and when we're old maids
We'll run in our underwear with our long braids
Down main streets in old Chicago, LA
Let all those punks see we have fun
Any age

Why Does Love
Hurt So Much

Why does it have to be like this?
A pounding in your chest, your hand forming a
fist,
You hit a wall to feel the pain
That in your mind you can't explain.
The years of text, of pencils raw
Cannot begin to teach the law
That love's a choice; not from the heart
But from a place that is less dark.

That growl of hunger in your gut
That comes from thoughts some say corrupt,
Some say are true, some just for fun.
But they are really a misrun,
A thought that is unfinished, quick,
That feels so good, but makes you sick.
It's not a feeling, in the same
Sense as you feel that twinge of shame
When one calls you a liar, thief.
Or in the way that you feel grief.
It is a choice, I say again,
But that does not decrease the pain.

I know it's hard to comprehend
How such a feeling can ascend
From such a place that is the mind.
The place that chooses cruel from kind.
The place that keeps that urge at bay.
The place that tells you what to say.
The place that lifts your hand to hit
That wall that you will not admit
Exists.
And yet, when it is struck
The noise that used to run amuck
Subsides. And all those songs you heard
That were all played at once, begird
Your mind, take over thoughts... They seize.

All's quiet now. All's calm. Serene.
But why deprive of such a scene
Your heart. Your mind. Your body, soul.
When all it craves is something more.
More of that feeling that's corrupt,
That's fun, that's true, that comes abrupt,
That takes over each bone, each cell
And come dawn, into life does swell.
Takes over every particle
Of light, of sound - a miracle.

Why would you pass on such a beam

Of pure perfection? Such a dream
That of a conscious mind arises,
And can be seen when day's despises,
Day's failures and day's successes
All take space in minds wide tresses.
A choice that never goes away.
Because, as you have heard me say,
Love is a choice. And while you can
Work on it, help it grow, you can't
choose when it falls into your life,
Your plans, your goals, sliced like a knife.
An unexpected visit, dropped
Into your lap, a wave unstopped.

But here's the question worth the world:
If love was lightly tossed, not hurled,
And hurt you less? Less tore your heart?
Would you still want it?

www.ingramcontent.com/pod-product-compliance
Lightning Source LLC
Chambersburg PA
CBHW070610160726
48003CB00005B/2209